Aesthetically Balanced

Aesthetically Balanced

From the Inside Out

Elle Edwards, FNP-C

Published by Tablo

TABLE OF CONTENTS

FORWARD

Dear Reader,

What you are about to read is a passion project set into motion with the intent to empower you, relate to you, and help you see the balance between the internal and external. It is meant to push you to dive deeper to truly see your worth, your wants, and uncover answers to questions you may be asking yourself. This book is a loving encouragement to help you get where you want to be. First through your soul, and then, aesthetically. The world of aesthetics is a balancing act, and one that has to be approached with grace and awareness. I hope after reading this you gain insight into how truly powerful, worthy, impactful, and complete you are. I hope you feel contentment and confidence in any aesthetic and life choices you embark on from here on out...

"Mental wellness is not a destination, but a process. It's about how you drive, not where you're going." - Author Unknown

With Respect and Love,
Elle xo

CHAPTER ONE

Internal + External = Balance

What is the impact of medical aesthetics and how does it relate to your own soul and personal growth?

I have worked in the world of medical aesthetics for over a decade. I have worked with plastic surgeons, dermatologists, inside spas and salons, and even owned my own practice doing exactly what this book is about, medical aesthetics.

I absolutely love what I do. I love being able to assist people in their journey of anti-aging, enhancing their confidence, and being able to replace deficits that naturally occur throughout our years. However, over the last few years, there has been a shift in energy within this industry. In hindsight, 2020 was not the most kind to us, and it weighed heavy on many individuals' mental state. Mental well-being can be categorized as anything from self-love to self-care and of course, self-esteem. I wanted to take the opportunity to reset us. To rewind, and get us back to the starting point where we each deserve to be. I hope to assist with a new momentum in gaining our power back in areas that may have been stripped from us. To attempt to shed light on areas of healing that we all need, and unite us on the foundation of simply being complete, worthy, and whole with no strings attached. Simply, just as we are.

Is this in any way to convince you never to enter the world of medical aesthetics or to stop doing what you're doing? Absolutely not. This is what I do for a living, and I wouldn't have it any other way. As an aesthetics provider, this shift in energy has made clear that not all money made is profitable, not if my patient leaves just as unbalanced as they came in as.

The world of medical aesthetics (fillers, neurotoxins, procedures, surgeries and everything in between), is something that came, saw and conquered our nation in what seems like an overnight phenomenon. The global aesthetic medical market size was estimated at $86.2 billion in 2020, and by 2028 it is predicted to reach 124.7 billion dollars (forbes.com). Why is that? Evolving technology in treatments and procedures plays a part, safety and availability along with more advanced research and education play into it as well. However, I think the personal state that each individual is in, is what has caused the aesthetics industry to skyrocket. Changing, altering or enhancing yourself in any way used to be rather taboo, judged, or thought to be dangerous. Now however, we see it as encouraged, expected, and required in many ways to keep up with the undeniable pressures of anti-aging. The idealism of how we should look, and the fear of simply accepting "ourselves" as is has become a daunting task.

In my opinion, this mindset starts when we were younger, and each year seems to increase in intensity. For instance, Oprah Winfrey conducted a survey and asked multiple questions about how women felt about their looks. She asked a group of teenagers and a group of women in their 60's. It was reported that 59.11% of teens admitted to using photo altering software to change the pictures people saw of them. 45% of teenagers are considering plastic surgery and almost 5% of those teenagers had already had plastic surgery. Looking at the National Organization of Women (NOW), their recent studies show that 53% of American girls are unhappy with their bodies, and that grows to 78% by the time the girls reach 17. Looking into the age range in which women typically come into medical aesthetics (college age), showed 70% of college women say that they feel worse about their own looks due to what is reflected in women's magazines and society.

These results are staggering, sad, and let's be honest, relatable to each and every one of us on some level. The world of medical aesthetics was intended to be such a beautiful opportunity for women to empower themselves in enhancing the beauty they had, receiving benefits of anti-aging, and heightening their confidence in everyday life. It was also set out to be a vessel to correct deformities, abnormalities, deficiencies, and other aesthetically altering situations that may have been out of the patients' control. That was always the goal, and still so important and wonderful to have the opportunity to offer. Sadly, somewhere along the road, like many things intended for pure good, things have gotten twisted into a new belief. That altering yourself is a necessity to make you whole, to give you self-confidence, to make you beautiful, and quite frankly, to make you enough and complete. Once created as icing on the cake, has also become the cake itself.

The lipstick effect is an instance I talk about quite often. It was something explained to me years and years ago by my sister who has worked in the fashion industry for the last 15 years (and is absolutely brilliant). The lipstick effect was coined after the Great Depression, which saw cosmetic sales rise in the four years from 1929 to 1933 (specifically, lipstick). Of all the things that would be deemed necessity, crucial, or even a luxury, lipstick may not be what most would assume for that time period or even today. To me, this truly speaks to the effect that the aesthetic world has on mental health, as well as the correlation of self-care and self-esteem. Think about the world renowned company, Estee Lauder. Founded by a husband and wife in the 1950's, Estee Lauder quickly grew to arguably one of the most desired cosmetic brands. It is still a household name to this very day. So what set them apart? What was their big break moment? Estee Lauder (the wife of Joseph Lauder), made the decision to be the first company to give out free samples/gifts with any purchase (giving away free product? WHAT?), and those samples/gifts were none other than beautiful miniature lipsticks. That's right! Many women would come back for that very same sample after they had opportunity to try it. The brilliant part? Most women would leave the shop having purchased much more than they originally planned for. When they returned home with their cream or blush, these women were transmitted into a feeling of a beauty, sexiness and a welcoming, uplifting change to their lips. For a moment in time, they were able to feel and see that special spark. They saw a reminder of the beauty, vibrancy and a life through a confident reflection.

Stress and trying times may affect everyone differently, but for women especially, those moments seem to be made bearable, better, or given hope by self-care in any form. Think about it, how much better do you feel when you get an opportunity to get dressed up and look your best? How much better is your mental health when your external, no matter how altered, looks like you're internal is feeling? Playing devil's advocate, how do you feel when you look beautiful and dolled up on the outside and have the worst day ever on the inside? Does it weigh on or diminish the way you feel you look? When you look at what you saw in the morning as a beautiful masterpiece, do you find ways to still pick it apart after not such a beautiful day? Chances are, yes. We all do. And that is because our internal beauty and self-esteem and self-worth must match our external. It must be a balanced relationship, and one that is worked on, protected and taken care of as one in the same. With that being said, you have to start somewhere to achieve that balance, and the first step is not always to work on the external, even though it might be much easier.

Where it starts to get tricky is understanding that your external worth, self-esteem and beauty needs to be this standard of you at any time and not just when you are at your best. When you strip away the filters, when you take off the makeup, when you remove the nice clothes, and are left with you; that is when you need to come to a point that you see the exact same level of worth. Now of course we can all appreciate when we do have those luxury's, and should it boost your self-esteem even more? Should you strut your stuff a little harder for that moment or that day or that date? Absolutely! But realize you need to be whole beforehand to be able to appreciate it for what it is, and that is simply the icing on the cake.

To say that mental health and medical aesthetics don't go hand in hand is to turn a blind eye and completely neglect the facts of relating internal and external completeness, and balanced aesthetics in general. It would be negligent to not realize the correlation between one's drive for perfection and where that truly stems from inside. I will tell you this, in my experience, the drive from the inside is not simply to enhance something. Typically, it goes much deeper, and more times than not, it's to change many things typically nothing to do with looks. Is part of that our job and responsibility as aesthetic providers to pick up on and decide whether we want to continue with treatment or not? Absolutely. But if we say no, someone else will always say yes, so speaking to every patient, woman, man, and reader, you must take it upon yourselves to seek out that aesthetic balance and completeness within yourself first. And yes, it starts with the internal.

The point of this book is not to detour you from continuing your journey with medical aesthetics. It is rather to take you back to the intended purposes of it. It is to give you your own power back and to align you with a self-love, self-worth, and overall contentment that you are whole to begin with. If you find that you may not be at that point quite yet, it is to provide pathways to help you get there. We can all get there, and we all deserve to. This book is also here to help guide you in a way of healing for those areas of need that may be hindering you. Not only hindering you from stepping into that healing and perspective, but more importantly, in believing it.

I encourage you to take notes, highlight areas that resonate with you, be open and honest with what you may discover about yourself. Be vulnerable and transparent, but above all be kind to yourself. This is something every person on earth struggles with and though it may be to different degrees, one thing you will learn is that it doesn't matter, because struggle is struggle, pain is pain, and the need for healing is universal. This book was written to get down to the nitty gritty, to be raw, and to provide a passageway to your next step forward in your journey of life. Whatever that may be. Utilize the tools at the end of the chapters, open your heart to resonate with the poems chosen for them, and give yourself the opportunity to meet yourself again with a blank slate and with the unbounding innocence, hope, and grace we all need and deserve.

"

We are all born so beautiful.
The greatest tragedy is being convinced we are not
-Rupi Kaur

CHAPTER TWO

Self-Esteem

Debunking the "if _____ then _____" way of thinking

Aesthetics in general is a game of balance, of shadow control, of replacing what is lost, and adding what we need to see as completion. If we add "this," then "that" will go away. If we take away this shadow, then this appears this way. It's all a balancing act. But what if we started looking at the way we are comparing internal and external, or having the expectations of such? If I get lip filler, then I will be more desirable to him. If I get Botox, then other people will think I am younger. If I get a new face, I won't be who I once was. This way of thinking sends you down a rabbit hole of misery. The external and internal both need to be balanced but they cannot balance each other out. Your internal needs to be healed by your internal and external can be enhanced by external. Combining the two as sisters when they are more like cousins once removed will only leave you feeling incomplete, unbalanced, and searching for the next thing to make it all better.

Injectables and the world of aesthetics is my passion. I love what I do, and I love enhancing the beauty in people, or even correcting the beautifully imperfect. Let me make clear one more time, this book is not to talk you out of enjoying self-care through aesthetics! Rather, to look at is as intended. For enjoyment of a relaxing facial or spa day, enhancement of deficits or small tweaks through treatments, *adding* to your confidence (not giving it to you), and assisting in making you happier with yourself (not others happier with you). Your external cannot fix, heal, or give your internal any completeness that is not already there. It simply can marry well with an already whole foundation and though it is something that is beautiful when you see brought to life, and so exciting to be able to create someone's dream aesthetic, not everyone has that whole foundation quite yet. Which means, not everyone is the best candidate and when I say that I don't mean because of anything on the external.

When it comes to consultations and procedures, I have probably turned away about 25% of the people who are seeking treatment. Why? Because ethically I cannot fulfill their request. There is a large mental health component to aesthetics. There is also a very interesting medical explanation for it, or rather for some. When we treat ourselves to something positive, our body releases endorphins which then triggers a positive feeling in the body similar to that of morphine. These endorphins interact with the receptors in your brain that reduce your perception of pain momentarily. Pain can be many things. You have physical pain or emotional pain. You can have constant pain or dull pain. All of which could be emotional or physical. Some of it may even overlap. Another interesting point is your body can only handle addressing one pain at a time. That's why we use distraction methods for needles such as tapping on the opposite shoulder or squeezing as hard as you can on a ball. This helps distract your mind into focusing on the new touch, or pain, no matter how dull it is verse what is truly happening and the true cause of it.

Much of what we do is a process and when you are going through this wonderful process, it can overshadow an unhealthy drive or pain or untreated wound, but they will always come back. This is why, when the healing process is done from any aesthetic treatment there's a sense of relief and then a period of elation and enjoyment and then inevitably either wanting more, thinking it was not enough, or finding something new to fixate on. You cannot fill, freeze, massage out, or cover internal turmoil, lack of self-esteem, trauma, or just plain and simple unhappiness. I assure you, it is a battle already lost as well as resources and time that could have been spent working towards the enhancement of soul and of treatment of the root issue that was truly needed in the first place.

Would you consider yourself the ideal candidate or patient for aesthetic treatments? Do you have a friend or family member that you think would be the worst? What, in your mind, do you feel distinguishes one from another? In my opinion, the best patients, or rather the best candidates for treatment, are the ones who truly are whole and who are coming in understanding that what they are doing is elective and that they are completely enough and whole without it but simply want to treat themselves by doing it for them. Not to give them happiness not to give them confidence not to give them a fill for a void, but rather to enhance all of those areas for themselves and themselves alone. What is interesting, is those are typically the patients who request less treatment and are more satisfied.

How Can You Learn to Break this Thinking?

How do you know if you are choosing to do something for the right reasons? How do you truly know if your decisions are being influenced by others or influenced by something deeper rooted within yourself? You are the best person to answer that. I am a big fan of lists. I make lists of things to do, things that need to get done, things I want to happen in the future, the lists of the lists continue on and on. Though I may take it to the extreme, when I need to check in with myself, I always resort to writing in some way. To me, writing it out is a way I can see it, touch it, hold it and reflect on it. It is a way I cannot hide from it; I cannot change the words that I'm seeing, it is a truth that is looking at me right in the face and one that I have to choose to face head on or not at all. A lot of times, we will ask ourselves questions, and then proceed to manipulate ourselves into giving us the answers we want. We can talk ourselves in or out of the exact same situation if we are not strongly planted in our own foundation. Especially if we don't truly know who we are and have healed ourselves from possible toxic ways of thinking or manipulations from the past either internally or with others. Learn to check in with your gut. If a decision is not easy, or does not seem 100% transparent with you, make sure you're asking the right questions. Not just the questions you know will get you to the decision, and not just the questions others may hurry along and ask, but the deeper ones. See if your answer changes.

You will notice at the end of this chapter I have attached a worksheet that I hope you find helpful if you are on the fence with your aesthetic journey. Being truthful and transparent to yourself is the only way you will get truthful and transparent answers back, and it is the only practice you will ever have in how your communications with others, and others with you, would be healthiest. Now that doesn't mean everybody should know your business, and I feel very much so the opposite. What it does mean, is that once you own your truth and decisions, and stand in it and are confident in it no one else will ever be able to sway you from it and you will never be ashamed of a decision you make moving forward especially in regard to how others perceive it.

That Self Love Glow

If we chose to love ourselves with the same intensity that we choose to worry about someone else loving us, we would all be in such a better place. Why is it that we look for outside sources to handle, fix or fill voids in an internal space that we only share with ourselves? That is our power. Why do we so freely give it away? And does it ever really stick? I have always been self-conscious of my eyes. I have very large eyes, I was teased a lot growing up about my eyes, and I've never really been 100% comfortable with the way they look. As an adult, I probably have a handful of people who will comment and say lovely things about my eyes on a weekly to monthly basis. It does feel good in the moment, it even has boosted my confidence and the very minimal times I wear makeup, I do try to play them up. But at the end of the day when my makeup is washed off, when my hair is up and I'm in my pajamas looking at no one but myself, do I like them any more than I did before all of the complements? Not really.

The important thing is I can appreciate the aspects I see within them. I am grateful that I share the same eyes as my dad, and the same color as my kids. I am blessed with excellent eyesight and healthy eyes in general. And the few times I do dress up for date nights I do love the way they look in makeup.

You don't have to love absolutely everything about you. None of us ever will, and that is perfectly okay! But getting to a place where you can still feel confident and appreciate your parts for all that they are is the ultimate goal. The moment you realize you don't need complements, (though they are nice to hear), I bet you won't feel the need to fix everything. When you can do absolutely nothing and look in the mirror and find appreciation and beauty and completeness. Only then will you realize that truly none of that comes from external alone. And at that time, if you choose to explore enhancing the things you love, tweaking things here and there or just preventatively, please do so!

It is a constant balance in the life of internal and external. If you eat nothing but unhealthy food it will catch up to you by ways of weight gain, skin disorders, along with internal struggles. If you cut on yourself or even pick at blemishes on your face you run the risk of infections internally, not just scars on the outside. There is a reaction for every action whether it be internal or external. The difference is, the external ones can be more easily healed, covered, altered, or justified. The internal ones take more time, self-realization, devotion, care, and concern. With that being said, the internal battles you win will be the ones the true glow up and breakthroughs come from. They will be the ones that transform you, that get people to notice your presence when you enter the room. Sure, your looks may get a glance and adoration, but your soul will be what gets the questions, the respect, and the loyalty. Invest in that. The external will be nothing more than a bonus.

My hope is that we can all get to a place where we realize we're talking about one whole being and not two separate entities. That is when, and only when, we can make a decision. It will at that point, be a decision that benefits that very whole and that is made in respects to it. In a world that is made to take away our self-love, my hope and want for each of you is that we use that to fuel a fire within us that is so powerful and so overwhelming that it sprouts a level of self-love that is unconditional, unshaken, and a force to be reckoned with. Each one of us is capable of it and was made to embody it, we just need to find where that went, what that looks like for us individually and why we haven't yet.

Your Gut Check - Aesthetic Version

- When did you FIRST start to think about doing this?
- What made you first think about it?
- Has anything influenced this decision?
- What would happen if you did not get this procedure?
- What do you feel you would gain by getting it and does that answer have to do with you or someone else?
- Is this attainable and maintainable?
- At the end of this, would this solve the first thought mention, or is it possibly deeper than that?

"

Stop breaking yourself into bite sized pieces to feed people.
Let them eat the whole cake
-unknown

CHAPTER THREE

The "WHY"

Are you doing this for the right reasons?

Before we dive in to our why, because let's be honest it's a little deep, let's just sit with the initial thought of the "what". Close your eyes, take a few deep breaths, and think of one specific moment that came to you within the last month, where you felt true, unabashed, joy and contentment. What did you feel about yourself in that moment? Do you remember the smells, or the weather, or the people around you? Now let's think about what started to alter that moment, and how much of it was under your control, how much of it was inevitable, and how much of that moment you held on to. Move on to your "what." Aka the treatment, procedure, life change, whatever it is that drove you to keep reading this book and look for answers to. Do you have it in your mind? Now, what is your why?

This can be asked with any decision we make. Why we choose to sleep instead of workout, why the smell of banana bread makes you feel at home, why you dye your hair one color over the other, the list can go on and on. One of the questions I'm always interested with patients coming in for aesthetic procedures is their "why". Some may think this is a simple question, but this is probably the question that most will have to take time to truly answer. Some of that may be that they would feel their answer would be judged, some of them truly don't know, some of them are ready with an answer with no issues at all, and some of them know their "why" and they know that maybe this isn't the answer but it's a band aid. If your why does not come to you right away, and is of positivity, encouragement and excitement, then maybe this isn't the answer to that particular why. Or at the very least, just not now. Maybe finding the true why and more importantly, the true answer to that why, is what is the vital first step.

The cause-and-effect have to balance. The risk-benefit has to balance. The want and what must at least even out. This is a difficult task when the input comes from the internal and the search for the output comes from the external. Now of course, this doesn't ring true 100% of the time, but it does for most cases. Like we discussed in chapter one, the internal and external are cousins once removed not sisters. If someone is on the fence or I feel as though there is more to it when it comes to getting a procedure done, I always recommend for them to stick with a consult and go home and write it all out. Write out what you would gain from this procedure, write out why you want this procedure and why you started to even begin to think about this procedure in the first place. Dive deep into what this decision will add to your life, your soul, and what it (if anything) may negatively be impacted. More times than not, I will not see that person back. Now it may be because they went to somebody else, but I hope it is because they are addressing the real issue before enhancing what they deem the solution.

Taking a plunge to alter, correct, or even enhance anything about the external aesthetics of oneself should be that person's own decision and their decision alone. It should be the finishing touches to an already complete dessert. Not because their spouse or mother or father or friend tell them they should get something done, but because they look in the mirror and know that they don't have to. Instead, they sure would like to. At the end of the day, you have power over your own body, and you need to make sure that you are respecting that power and placing it truly in the areas that best suits it, best grows it, and best completes it with respect to internal and external. The minute you give away that power to a person, to society, or even to yourself in a negative way, is the moment that power turns from *empowerment* to power *over* you and that is something that is very difficult for anyone to take back for themselves.

Time is best spent in growth and moving forward, in happiness, and in setting a constant new bar and new goal to reach. You cannot do that by cutting corners and trying to mask, or in this case, fill around the true "why". You also cannot do that when you are trying to gain all of those things through the pleasing of others. And what will become even more interesting to each one of you, is the more exclusive you become to yourself and your own wants and your own goals and your own confidence and whatever that may mean to you ...the more people will be drawn to you. When you try to people please, keep up with somebody else's definition of confidence or beauty or what goals you should be doing or what you're great at, they will never see your value or respect it, they will only see your incompletion and debt to their idea of you. One thing I have learned, is the more I protect my energy and respect my boundaries the more people come correct to meet me at that line, because they then realize that their view of my value and happiness and truly even their opinion or judgment will absolutely never hold any worth in comparison to my own about myself. There is nothing wrong with that, and that may be hard for family members and those close to you to fully accept, but the ones who deserve to be there will always support and adapt alongside this new and balanced you. Who knows, you may even be the one to start a new and healthier trend in communication and boundaries for your family, friends, and the next generation to come. Never underestimate your power.

“

Speaking of your power, please remember this. Remember that you don't have to set yourself on fire to keep others warm. Your only responsibility in a relationship of any type whether it be with yourself or with someone else, is to love, accept, grow, hold and stay accountable to, and be honest.

If you are standing in these powerful guidelines of love and relationship and someone else finds fault in it, that is fault they are and were already looking for. Trust me, they would have found something in some way, shape, or form regardless. One thing I find interesting is when I'm told an opinion or a story or a judgement from somebody and that doesn't necessarily match up with the person whom I know they're speaking about or I simply do not know the other person well enough to make a judgement; I always go directly to that person if at all possible when it comes to matters that will affect my decisions going forward. I do this, because I want us all to remember, there's "his side, her side, and then the truth" in most cases. I never cast a judgment on anybody based on somebody else's word or story no matter the source. And if somebody does, it's because deep rooted they were hoping that that person was like that for their own reasons whether it be jealousy, intimidation, or just unhappiness within themselves. We must hold ourselves to the same standard. If someone is making you to believe you should change internally or externally, challenge their motive. Is it something that is profitable to your soul internally that you too see as maybe something that needs to be strengthened or does it more benefit the situation and them? If it has to do with the external, is this something that they are mirroring your concerns about and helping you come to the best decision for you or is this something that they are seeing, and you are simply mirroring their sight and not your own. Never let someone else's whys become your own or influence the decisions you personally make. You are absolutely capable of making them yourself.

What Were My Why's?

One of the most frequently asked questions I get is, *"What have you had done?"* I always like to rephrase that too, *"What enhancements did I make to meet my goals."*

What were my why's and how did I get those why's answered? For me, at the end of the day it's not about just getting stuff done, it's about being aesthetically balanced, which is the whole point of this book. When people look at me, it may not look like I have done anything, or it may look like I've done a lot, it really depends on where the person is in their own journey and not where I am. What I find is when an individual is comfortable in themselves, they tend to not piece apart someone else's journey, looks or personal aesthetic choices. They just see them as a complete package because they see themselves as a complete package from the start. When they are not complete or possibly insecure about the choices they have made or are making or just in general with themselves, they desperately want to see that in someone else. I will give you an example.

I was signed to two modeling contracts for a total of four years. Not one day of it did I feel I deserved to be there or hold the title of "model" and was always shocked when anyone booked me. What was more interesting, was my whole life people had told me I should model. This of course is deemed to be a great compliment and I appreciated it each time. Little did others know, where I was with myself in my own life, I didn't believe or see it at all. What absolutely blew my mind (and I did not understand the reasoning until now), is when I actually became a model, how quickly the same people who told me I should be one, started to piece apart who I actually was. I got a lot of comments like, "well, I mean she's pretty, but she's not that pretty." Odd right? especially because prior to me signing, that is the opposite of what these same individuals shared with me. Some people will support you, encourage you, and root you on until you get to a level that makes them uncomfortable. A level that makes them feel it outweighs theirs, whether you intend to make them feel that way or not. And when that happens, it's like a switch that will be flipped. That is not a reflection of you, and that does not mean that you do not deserve absolutely every ounce of any success that comes your way. We are all deserving of success, love, gains of any kind, just in our own ways and those ways that are meant for us individually.

Same can be said when it pertains to your own whys in medical aesthetics. Many people may try to talk you out of it for reasons such as their own jealousy, their own insecurities, that you are doing something that maybe they cannot, or simply lack of education on the subject. There are numerous reasons. I often get patient after patient who will tell me how others will say they are only pretty BECAUSE of the treatments they get. Who says that? Let me be the one to tell you, you are pretty before, during, after and beyond that. You will always be prettier (inside and out) than a comment like that. Why do we care so much about other people's how's, but never about their whys? Why do we so quickly judge, justify, and discount and so rarely edify, genuinely enquire about, and encourage? Why does one feel as though it would take away from them to do so freely for others even though we all want that done to ourselves? On the opposite end of the line, and even more so, why not consider what can you yourself possibly GAIN by doing so rather than loose? Pretty is pretty. It doesn't matter the how, what, or why. One thing that will make anyone less pretty is their internal. So once again...invest and get settled with the internal first.

The thing about being yourself, and being balanced at the same time, is that you will see that everyone around you can succeed. Through beauty, education, fitness, motherhood, in any possible way. By knowing yourself, you will see that others can meet all of these milestones and achieve all the beautiful goals without one ounce of that success taking away from your own path, in your own individual ways. It also does not mean you are less than them or in competition with them. You can be happy and encouraging and supportive and root somebody else on without it taking away from you. There is room for all of us to be beautiful no matter how that is manifested in the world whether it be modeling, whether it be just knowing and feeling that beauty, whether it be making a beautiful impact on the world through who you are and your craft.

Someone else's beauty will never take away from yours. So support them, see their accomplishments as their accomplishments. We should be that for one another. We should be everyone's biggest fan. But also remember, you can only be that when you are your own first and when you realize you are not in competition with any other person in this world but yourself. Even deeper than that, it is not a competition with yourself that you are in rather an accountability to continue to have the desire to evolve, reinvent yourself and grow.

❝

On the other side of things, if you are feeling the need to dim your light so that others' lights look brighter and they feel more comfortable in that room, please stop. If you want to be "extra", or dress up for every occasion, or switch careers, or do a fitness competition, or write a book, don't let anyone allow you to feel you should not. Step into that success and own it.

One thing I've been told by a small handful of individuals before, is that I am difficult to have a relationship with because I'm intimidating. Mind you this comes from people who haven't really tried to talk to me, but their reasoning is that I'm intimidating and thought of myself as better. This came after multiple times assuring them that, in fact, was not how I felt in the slightest nor how I ever would feel. It was something I sat with for a while and then I read a quote that just said, *are you intimidating or are they intimidated.* Because there is a difference. I realized I was not intimidating at all, they were intimidated by what they didn't understand, what they viewed as competition, and certain levels that they themselves viewed as making theirs look less than, which in all reality did not, we were simply just on different paths, and in very different stages of life.

❝

You cannot compare apples and oranges in life. You cannot compete where you don't compare.

This is not meant as a putdown. My daughter has phenomenal curly beautiful hair, and my son has thick luscious straight here. I cannot compare the beauty, the appearance, which one is better or worse, the growth patterns, any of it because they are two completely different things. You cannot compare a leading defense lawyer's journey with a grocery store manager's journey. But what you need to realize, is that both can be equally successful, just within their own path. Just like both my children's hairs can be equally beautiful, and I would equally not change a hair on either's heads. You have to look at the bigger picture and realize everybody's level of success, of goals, of finances, of one's own drives in life can be all over the board but who are you and who are any of us to start piecing apart what is better than the next or what is more important than the next or why somebody is successful and whether they deserve that. Look at all of that wasted time and energy. I mean truly think of how silly that is. Does any of it affect you, no.

We can all be successful, and beautiful, without comparison. To each their own. So, if you are feeling that someone is doing that to you, do not dim that light. If anything, get a brighter bulb and turn that on and stand in it because you deserve to be there and you deserve to be proud of yourself. You deserve to feel like you have earned it. You are not bragging by being who you are, and you are not being extra by doing things your way as long as your intent is good and pure, and your heart is right. Nobody should make you feel like you should ever be muted in action, in speech or in any other way.

With that in mind, let's take a look at my journey both internally and externally and break down my "why's".

INTERNALLY:

What have I done, and continue to do to heal and grow my soul?

- Therapy for Trauma and PTSD for 3 years
- Group Therapy for 3 years
- Family Counseling for 1 year
- Dove into my faith and grabbed hold with a grip I'll never loosen
- Read devotionals on how to better myself as a parent, as a spouse, as a woman, and as a person monthly
- I have learned to be quick to love, quick to remove toxic energy and behavior completely, and always open to forgiveness and reconciliation
- Extensive work on self-love, accountability, and letting go of what I cannot control
- Still working on severe anxiety through personal check ins, journaling, reading, and even through writing this book
- Obtained a macro coach to help me with my relationship with food and keep me on track
- Obtained gym equipment to utilize working out in my home as a form of therapy and make me feel strong and healthy

EXTERNALLY:

How have I put the finishing touches on my aesthetic journey after the internal was on track?

- Every 6-8 weeks: Facial, hair/nails
- Quarterly: Botox and micro-needling
- Once a year: Deep peel and filler to add to the again deficits we all get
- I have had my teeth worked on to remove damage caused by eating issues in my past and chips due to trauma

- I have had reconstruction surgery on my face due to trauma caused when I was younger
- I had all tattoos removed due to starting over with new meaning and intention
- I get my eyebrows micro-bladed yearly (And they are fabulous)

Now it's your turn. Let's pause and have you take a moment to write what you are currently doing (or would like to do) for yourself both internally and externally

Reading this, that may seem like a lot to some. Well, it's the perfect amount for me. But if there is judgment behind that assumption, that might be part of the bigger problem. To be quite honest, I am worthy of and deserve everything I've done for myself. I have no issue saying all these things because they come from a healthy place and they come from a completely balanced being that I could not be prouder of. If you really wrote out everything you do that in some way affects your aesthetic balance, I think we would all be shocked at how much more it is then you actually think.

The difference is, when it's something that's not healthy we tend to put it in a different category and not realize that it is a part of the balance or rather imbalance that we are committing to. If you are a heavy drinker or go on shopping sprees that land you in debt or find yourself clicking the buy button online every time you feel a bit off, that is a behavior pattern directly correlated to your aesthetic balance. That still gets added to your list. Everything we do somehow is tied into our own self-love or self-hate and should be accounted for. I could easily rip apart my own list and justify a lot of those as necessities. Such as nails, hair and even facials, (because much of my career is about appearance and preservation). But instead of trying to justify it, I am confident in standing in it because I am whole without it, but it makes me happy to have and there's nothing wrong with that. Stop making justifications, excuses, or belittling yourself for fear of judgment and realize that their judgment comes from their own unresolved issues.

Another story for some perspective. I once purchased a designer purse (funny because I rarely wear purses, but wanted to have one elegant one), I remember people saying that it was a waste of money and I was being "flashy," and that my values were off. Here's the thing. I do not know your financial bracket, income, or budget. You do not know mine. You also don't know how or why I obtained the purse. I had made a personal goal of opening my own practice and paying off the debt myself for it and worked hard to meet that goal. When I did, I rewarded myself with a purse. The point is, we often negate the need of an explanation for something positive. The cost of things is all relative to each and every person. If you're honest with yourself, if you could continue to enhance yourself, if you could do more (with activities, financial planning), you would. Sure, maybe it wouldn't be in terms of a purse. Maybe it would be setting up a savings account, or your kids college fund, or renovating a piece of a house, or dressing up and going to a fancy dinner, but whatever it is, that's your reward, your goal, and your plan and it's a great one and you deserve it. And who is to say the person getting a purse doesn't already have those other things or simply will make those things their next goal? Again, we don't know everyone's achievements, goals, planning, grind, or anything past what they display so let's all be a little kinder and give each other the benefit of the doubt. At the end of the day, it does not affect you, take away from you, or mean you have to do it or can't do it.

Unwarranted judgements in general come from your own self-hate, jealousy and insecurity. I say this to encourage you to revert back to what we discussed earlier in this chapter and realize we all are on our own journey; we all are deserving of it all, but it takes away from it when you justify things to yourself and when you pick apart those judgements of others.

If you recognize that you have said those things to someone in the past, guess what, you are human and this is not meant to make you feel bad. Instead, I encourage you to dive deeper in yourself, to see why you feel the need to do so and where that comes from in your own healing. If you have received this judgment in life, you are also human. This is not to boast about how right you are in your position, rather to make you empathetic to those making the judgments and also to just confirm that it's not a reflection of you and your journey. One thing I try to do is never make a side fully right and a side fully wrong. Because truly it's subjective and at the end of the day a lot of where we stand comes from where we are at with ourselves. One thing I say quite a bit in any time of indifference is that the number one communication error is people equating taking accountability with taking blame.

Let's read that again. One of the most common communication and relationship errors is equating taking accountability with taking blame. They are different. If this doesn't resonate with you now, it will as your journey through healing matures. Let this be a seed planted.

"

One day you will tell your story of how you overcame what you went through
and it will be someone else's survival guide
-Brene Brown

CHAPTER FOUR

Your Reflection

What truly is it that you are seeing?

Let's start this chapter by looking at ourselves in the mirror and saying one thing we truly love about ourselves. First, internally with who we are and then externally what we love about ourselves when we look at our reflection.

Many of us can pinpoint exactly what we do not like about our looks, even ourselves. Things we would change either aesthetically or personality wise and it all comes very easy for us to do so. What are you truly seeing in those things that you dislike? Do you dislike your nose because when you look at it you always have disliked it, or do you dislike your nose because your ex-boyfriend or classmates made you self-conscious of it? Do you dislike your lips because you truly just find larger lips more attractive to you, or do you dislike them because you feel as though you are not sexy without them? Are you truly seeing things that justify being altered and that will actually fix or enhance a healthy desire to do so, or are you trying to fix something to heal a deeper wound or insecurity? Because let me tell you, if you get bigger lips but you as a person are still insecure and don't feel sexy, you're just going to feel unsexy with big lips.

Understanding whether you are seeing something that can truly be enhanced to solve a minor issue or slight dislike... OR seeing something under the surface that you think a quick fix will alter the entire emotional state of, are two very different things. One of which is a long-lasting joy and one of which is simply pressing pause on the emotional bleeding behind it. Diving into reflection can be broken into three main categories. Personal or Self-reflection, Perceived reflection, and Cultural perception. All of which must be respected for what they are and how they add and take away from your wholeness and balance.

Personal/Self Reflection

I have never been someone who can relate with feeling or embodying "sexy". That is not a personality or emotional trait that I personally resonate with, but that does not have any reflection on my attractiveness. It's just simply who I am, my confidence and my attractiveness are shown differently. When I am in workout clothes, I feel most confident but when I try to dress as how I think I "should" dress or keep up with others' standards of dress, I may look prettier but because of how uncomfortable I feel inside I will never truly embody the beauty of that outfit nor will I feel it.

"

Gut check: what are you wearing, doing, feeling, tasting, smelling when you feel your most true, authentic, real self?

Confidence, contentment, and knowing who you are and what you're comfortable with will truly amplify any beauty you can think of. No one person is for everybody. Just like when you find your spouse or a love interest, you are most likely attracted to them and think that they are the absolute best pick. Your best friend may think the exact opposite. And both of you are right. Out of the millions of people in this world you do not have to be everyone's "the one', or even liked by everybody. You have to be enough for yourself and yourself only and when you are, it will give you a vision to see those who in turn see that in you, and if it's meant to be, that person who sees that in you, will also be the one you see for you too.

Your personal reflection is also highly influenced by your mental state and where you stand with yourself. You could be the most prim and proper, beautiful, organized, brilliant, have it all together person but if you are in agony on the inside or have unresolved issues or trauma or just simply are not happy you will never see your reflection for what it is and quite honestly neither will anybody else. There is something to be said about how one carries themselves. That is something you cannot fake. You can fake being happy, you can fake keeping it all together for some time, and you can fake it all for the gram but what you cannot fake is that presence of someone who walks in the room and truly knows his or her own power and embraces it in a humble and eloquent way because he or she knows that it's one that never has to be proven, especially to others. Working on the internal reflection will change, magnify, and give you 20/20 on the external without ever touching or changing anything tangible.

Perceived Reflection

For this section, I'm going to use the most common example I can think of. Many times, I see friends, even some friends that I've had, press their ideals of what a man should be onto one another and even steer them so far away from what probably was what was best for them simply because it is not best for that friend. We all value different things in relationships. Relationships with ourselves are no different and neither is how we choose to see the ones we want to have with others. There are so many different views and values and expectations. So many levels that we all are trying to meet, but the only ones that truly matter are your own. If we could all just respect those of others instead of speaking ours as if they are right or as if people would be better off with them and while we are at it, if we could also stop listening to others thinking that maybe we don't know what's best for ourselves or maybe we would be better off if we adapted to somebody else's ideologies and standards, I truly believe we would all be a better society and one that would be much more accepting, loving and uplifting to one another. And to be quite honest, happier and less stressed in general.

It is hard enough in this world to be kind to ourselves, but when you add a layer of never being able to meet all of this world's expectations, it becomes impossible. Even the fear of meeting those closest to you who are supposed to be your biggest supporters' expectations can be stressful, which is absolutely crazy. Stick to your path, your foundation, your visions of both yourself and your relationships. And if your path isn't currently healthy and one that is meeting your own fulfillment, dreams, goals and standards that you know you should have for yourself then change it and never look back.

Your friends and family can still be walking right beside you, they're just simply on a path that may look different and that's OK for both sides. It is the same with us. I have had people walking right beside me, still feel the need for me to be holding their hand on *their* path for *mine* to be successful. Even with very simple things such as telling me to let my hair grow as long as possible and I look so great this way or that way or I should go back to doing this or stop doing that. Not that I need to explain my decisions to anyone, especially my aesthetic ones, but I feel very feminine, confident, and comfortable with my hair a little bit shorter. I feel best in comfortable casual clothes and minimal makeup. I have tried every which way of people's ideas of how I will be at my best and the truth is I am only at my best when I am myself. And whatever that may look like I'm so content with and it gives me so much confidence and power that that beauty is immeasurable to other people's ideas or wishes for me. Because at the end of the day I need to love who I look like in the mirror and who I know I am down to my core. Them loving what I look like or me as a person, is not going to influence my energy, change my soul or help me grow and love myself. I would encourage you all to try to get to that point because when I tell you the freedom that comes along with it is the largest weight that will get lifted off of your shoulders, it truly is.

Cultural Reflections

America is a melting pot. If you travel outside the country and immerse yourself in a new one, and experience all of the new things around you, you will notice that America is one of the only ones where you can be in a room and every single person is completely different in culture and belief. There is a beauty in that, and that is one of the amazing things about America. But that also brings up some issues that need to be addressed. Cultural reflection also needs to be considered and taken into account on one's own journey as well as be respected by your peers throughout it.

Just because somebody is living in America that does not mean that their cultural foundation is yours. There is not one culture, there is not one foundation, there is not one way to be. I find in relationships that involve different cultures or even friendships, sometimes that line can be blurred and judgments and pressures to conform to somebody else's culture ends up derailing one from their own. That could be detrimental to the soul on so many levels.

Each culture has their own idea of the best makeup look, their own pallet of fragrances that are appealing, food that they may find delicious, and their own take on how they view exercise, nutrition and what they deem appropriate with dress. Now yes, these particular things are all simply to do with aesthetics, but the difference both internally and spiritually would take up an entire chapter itself so I am sticking to the basics. The vast number of different cultures living in America still each have their own cultural beliefs on all of these subjects. That is why, telling somebody who is of a different cultural background to conform to your view of what their reflection should be based on your own, may not be the best way to go. Nor is it okay for someone to try to convince you of that. There is no right way to look or feel about yourself and no wrong way to look and feel about yourself unless it's one stuck in self-hate. Just something to keep in mind for those seeking advice from others or those giving it, making sure you understand their (your own) cultural preferences and guidelines and pay respect those as well.

If you think about it, sometimes even changing a hairstyle for somebody can be life altering. Imagine having to change your entire view on your own culture. I have four best friends. Every single one of them is from a different cultural background and when I say different, I mean wildly different. I absolutely love when we talk about how we're feeling towards our relationships, how we feel about the way we look, how we view success, even down to something as silly as what we are all wearing for certain special occasions. I love it because it is always so different and so across the board but absolutely every piece of it, is right. And when one of us may get in a bind and ask for help whether it be a problem with our spouse or a problem with our family, what I have found is how I would solve it or recommend solving it may be inappropriate to some of their cultural beliefs. Who am I to say that that's right or wrong.

Instead, I need to take it upon myself to educate myself in being culturally sensitive so that I can still be that soundboard for them and help support them in the way that best suits their beliefs, their soul, and the reflection of their culture. Isn't that what we should all do in any relationship? Is to meet the person where they are at, in who they currently are and just be there to, yes, hold them accountable but also help them grow in the path that they themselves have chosen to be on and in a way that benefits their own cultural reflection and belief system regardless of what ours is. This may hit a nerve with a lot of the readers, but all I'm asking is for us to get to a place where we realize our way is not the only way and it's certainly not the "right" way. It is simply *our* way and what is right for ourselves. That should definitely be embraced and not altered and not changed but with the same reverence and respect neither should somebody else's. And nobody should be made to feel as though it should.

If you're reading this, and you are the one on the receiving end of feeling the need to turn from your own cultural reflection let me be here to tell you that if you do, it needs to be because your beliefs have changed and by your own accord. Not because anybody else said something, not because you are being made to feel less than or less worthy or like you will never get to A, B or C without it. Each culture and cultural reflection are of equal need, equal importance, and deserves the respect in seeing the power behind it. Do not ever change who you are for any other reason but tweaking it to strengthen growth through your own eyes and with your own goals, desires, beliefs and self-worth in mind. The only relationship you have forever is with yourself and your higher power, which I say a lot, but it is true and that is the one you need to be held accountable to. So, make sure your decisions are ones that are made in a deliberate and wholehearted way and not one that you will look back on with doubt, questions, or regret.

My Experience with Reflections Globally
and How it has Impacted Mine

My family is made up of many different cultures. I am Mexican, my grandmother being from Mexico as well as German, and a small percentage of Native American. My husband is also of mixed race with completely different cultural background than mine. So, in our household we have a lot of different cultural reflections that come into play, but we find so much beauty in it. On top of that, we have spent the last eight years living between America and Japan for my husband's career. For anyone who has lived in other countries it is interesting to see what they value about themselves and in relationships verse Americans. Living in Japan, it has been such an eye opening and humble experience to understand their values of themselves, finances, parenting and relationships, aesthetics and learn to see it from their perspective, respect it, and intern it has grown my own in different ways. I feel as though I can sum up how it has changed me with five simple points.

1. We need a lot less than we think
2. Appreciation for the efficiency and short cuts we have in America
3. When you have time, be present in it and indulge in it
4. There will always be debt, but not always one another
5. Don't dwell on negative moments when a positive forever can be so much better

We need a lot less than we think. One of the most interesting things of watching COVID-19 happen where I live in Arizona and watching it in Japan was just this very mindset. When things happened here, people were out of toilet paper for weeks to months in some areas, masks all of a sudden skyrocketed in prices as well as gloves and hand sanitizer, it turned one group of people against another based on their belief system. People rebelled against suggestions based on their own rights and others turned on their own families or friends based on their stances. It was truly madness no matter which side of what you stood on.

When I landed in Japan, I was expecting something similar, and saw something completely different. Masks were discounted in price at times down to $1.00 USD so that everybody made sure that they had what they needed and if you forgot a mask (happened to me on more than one occasion) people were readily available and wanted to give you one to help you out. There was not anything out of stock because their mindset was why would we take more than what we need because other people need it too. Even if they didn't believe in wearing masks, they just wore them because it made other people feel better about the situation and it showed comradery that we were all in this together regardless of how silly some felt about it. It was a mindset of being a team even if every player had their own thoughts that differed. It was about considering others and knowing that if you were in need, they would then consider you as well. This way of thinking is something I have tried to adapt to and just one of the many ways that has changed me.

The houses in Japan are much smaller and I have always been so concerned that our kids don't have enough space, that they wouldn't have room for all their toys, and that I could never really get comfortable. We don't have a dishwasher, their washer and dryer situation are less than comparable, and there's no true backyard or front yard. If you ask my kids where they have more fun 10 out of 10 times their answer is Japan. It has forced us to not rely on ease but rather rely on each other. They have built up parks and open fields and creeks and every outdoor commodity you could think of for kids to grow and play with one another and appreciate the beautiful world that we all live in. As much as I don't like doing dishes, we have a system down and it only takes maybe 10 extra minutes. The kids don't have nearly the same number of toys but play so much harder and so much more joyful there then they do when they're surrounded by 100 toys because it's a time, we are all together. It's truly quality over quantity and though when we come home, we appreciate everything we have here and yes in a lot of ways it's much more comfortable but in a lot of ways all it is, is space and things. Sometimes I feel like it even takes us away from diving into that closeness we have in Japan, all together. So Simply put, in any aspect of the phrase we do need a lot less than we think.

Though point 2 I think is self-explanatory 3, 4 and 5 really all overlap with one another. Workdays and school days in Japan are something I've never seen. Kids will leave the house bright and early and not return till 8:00 PM or later sometimes. They don't get summer break the same as we do, and they don't get all the breaks in between. Adult's work is equally as grueling. But when they have Holidays or days off, I've never seen such grasping of joy and fulfillment and the need to truly embrace it and be present in it. They travel, they take day trips, they explore their own country, they explore surrounding ones, or they just be in the moment with their loved ones and enjoy each moment of their time that they have.

My husband and I have always tried to limit the amount of debt that we have and truly not have any. It's always been our goal and when we make decisions, I do find us looking more so at the price tag and maybe not really grasping what the experience would be or how it would add to our relationship as a family, with each other, and our own self growth. I've asked many people in Japan how they are OK with taking on so much debt or how they're finding it possible to go on all of these trips and do all of these things and I find that their look back to me is one of complete shock as to how I would not understand.

They have a mindset of making the most of the little time they have regardless of the momentary cost because at the end of the day that's why they're working so hard. Don't get me wrong, I'm still a believer that you should limit debt and I will always have a strict budget, but I have tried to view things from a different mindset of risk verse benefits in the sense of, if it is something that would benefit our soul, our growth and our quality as an individual, a married couple, and as a family I have found that I have let that trump the amount, if possible.

Lastly, not dwelling on moments but rather fixating on how great the future will be. This is by far the toughest lesson I have learned and one I still struggle with committing to daily. I struggle with a lot of anxiety and I am a worrier by nature. It's definitely to an unhealthy level and I have always tried to work on it, but it is something I will work on forever, most likely. What I have learned through multiple discussions while in Japan, is that maybe dwelling on certain moments or certain fears are keeping my eyes blind to the good that could come from them or causing me to take a longer road to the happiness on the other side. Things happen. But I have learned to try to see the forest through the trees and at the end of the day that one hour of unpleasantness means nothing to the 23 that were great. That a year or two of bad memories or poor decision-making or whatever it may be is really nothing in the span of your future. And even deeper than that, you don't know how long your future is going to last, so wouldn't you want to make the most of it. Wouldn't you want to reflect on the good and the joy and the love and hold yourself to a standard of staying in that energy and amongst only those who share in it and add to it, for however long you can.

My husband and I have never really gotten into a true fight though we disagree and at times can get on each other's nerves. Whenever something arises, I always ask is this something that would truly end our relationship? 10 times out of 10 it is not, so in my mind that already takes the point of fighting out of the equation. At that point, that situation truly becomes one of okay, this is where we are at so how we are going to work through this. What needs to happen to where we can get through this together, learn what we need to learn, change what needs to be changed, and move on. That has been a game changer from the start and one that trickles down to every relationship in my life including setting that example of open, vulnerable, and accountable communication with my children. You can still feel every single feeling and that be validated without having to express it in an unhealthy way. Him and I are on the same team, ALWAYS, so why fight against it and not for it to win?

I know a lot of this has veered away from your soul, your aesthetics and your balance, but it speaks very directly to the wholeness of your life. And unfortunately, it takes only one weak part of your life to slowly start to chip away at even the strongest parts. So, throughout your journey of wellness, self-growth, self-love, and internal and external aesthetics you would be amazed at how the change of your mindset will start opening up new areas of your life outside of that, that you then start to also grow and shape and elevate. You will learn new boundaries, healthy boundaries and hopefully even create new goals and dreams as well based upon the new you, you are evolving into. Life is such a journey and has so many twists and turns and rivers and valleys and ups and downs and it will be ever evolving within you and around you and what a beautiful and empowering ride that can be if we just let it.

Journey of Life

Author Unknown

Do not undermine your worth by comparing yourself with others,
It is because we are different that each of us is special.
Do not set your goals by what other people deem important.
Only you know what is best for you.
Do not take for granted the things closest to your heart.
Cling to them as you would your life,
for without them, life is meaningless
Do not let your life slip through your fingers
By living in the past nor for the future.
By living your life one day at a time,
You live all the days of your life.
Do not give up when you still have something to give.
Nothing is really over until the moment you stop trying.
It is a fragile thread that binds is to each other.
Do not be afraid to encounter risks.
It is by taking chances that we learn how to be brave.
Do not shut out of your life by saying it is impossible to find.
The quickest way to receive love is to give love;
The fastest way to loose love is to hold it too tightly.
In addition, the best way to keep love is to give it wings.
Do not dismiss your dreams.
To be without dreams is to be without hope;
To be without hope is to be without purpose.
Do not run through life so fast that you forget
not only where you have been, but also where you are going.
Life is not a race, but a journey to be savored each step of the way.

CHAPTER FIVE

But what do you LOVE?

Changing the mindset of fixating on what you "hate" and instead enhancing what you love and not being swayed in it

When I first transitioned from working in dermatology to working in medical aesthetics, I was trained by the best, as we all should be. For me, the best was where I currently work at Institute of Aesthetics. Jennifer Prince and Brandie Henderson, who were my mentors, trained me to start every consult by asking my patient what three things they love about their looks before even discussing what brought them in to the consult. I learned that if my patient could not name one thing, that was a red flag not to treat them, or at least not at that visit. That was such a big moment in my own healing and something I have carried with me for every single patient that sits in my chair. Being able to love yourself and openly embrace sharing that love without fear of judgment is one of the most powerful things a woman can do. If you cannot name three things you love about yourself, nothing I can do in that chair is going to give you that love. It will give you a sense of relief for a moment in time. But it will not create the self-love that only you can create internally.

Of course, there are exceptions such as injury or trauma and there can be a true deficit or issue that we need to address specifically. That does not overshadow the love you should have for yourself in other areas. Whether there is a true issue we are correcting or not, self-love is self-love and if you cannot list three things out of the thousands of things other people might be able to see in you or say about you, then

the number one issue to address is not the external one bringing you to
that chair.

" "

Before you make a consultation for anything and with anyone, I encourage you
to look in the mirror and say three things you love about the general area that
you are looking to change.

If you find it difficult, go back to your why. If you find it easy,
appreciate those areas over the next few days even more. Say it again
and see if your mindset changes in terms of goals, wants, and needs of
treatment. There is no right or wrong in this situation. If they do not
change then great, book that appointment and go get enhanced. If they
do change, then that is simply enough of an enhancement, and now
it's on to the next goal. I find the most important way of assessing any
need, want, or desire is simply checking in with yourself. This helps
us stay in-tune with that balance between internal and external and
what you truly need while still moving forward and being deliberate and
intentional in those moves.

I have always been long and lean and never with too much body
to me. Most of my adult life, it has been drilled into me, that my
body needs to change. Instead of jumping on this bandwagon with
trying to keep up with the latest celebrity trends, body dysmorphic
thinking, or the pressures of society and what is "in" right now, I did
something different. I took my own advice. I started dressing in ways
that accentuated the strength of my body. I have always been more
muscular and when I saw how my body looked in certain clothes it
made me feel strong and empowered and beautiful and sexy and all of
the things some had told me would only come from being curvier.

On the opposite end of the spectrum, one of my good friends is
a beautiful curvy woman who has always wanted to be fit and thin.

She accepted the same challenge and she started to dress in ways that accentuated her curves in a more appealing way to her and by the end of this little experiment we did, we both realized how much we truly love our bodies. How much they represented who we were and give us a sense of pride and confidence that we did not have prior to.

There is no right or wrong body. There is healthy, there is strength, there is beauty, there is sexiness, and all of these things are different for each and every eye. Beyond that, the most vital eye to be accepted, loved, nurtured, and desired is your very own. It goes back to that self-love glow. The body that embodies standing in all it's glory. We all have it, we all deserve it, and though the road to finding it may be a winding one with some veering curves here and there, we are all entitled to our own unique one that was built from love.

❝

Instead of rushing to solutions of how you think you need to be, change your mindset. To simply love what you have and embody it. Stand in who you are, where you are, what you are, in this very moment and love on it so fiercely that your negativity has no choice but to submit to it.

Will this work for everything? Absolutely not. But it will work for a lot of it. If you don't like a facial feature, try playing it up with a bold eye or structured blazer and see how that changes your mindset. If you don't like your shyness, role play situations before you enter them and just give yourself the gift of being a little more prepared. You do not have to change yourself to fix some "problem' you don't have. You need to love yourself to see the beauty of who you are and learn new ways to love that about you. If you're curvy and love your curves but still want to get fit, great do that! If you are lean and love that but still want to put on some muscle and achieve some shape and strength, then great, do that! If you accept and love your lips for what they are but still want to go bigger, I got you! By all means have goals and continue to improve and enhance yourself in any capacity but just know that it will never bring you peace unless you start from a place of full acceptance of your starting point. One that is full of self-love and not self-hate.

What if you don't know what you love and you don't know how to find out? At times of life, slumps happen. Whether it be circumstances, we lose who we are, what we love, our beliefs change, or even where we stand in certain topics. You can be in a place in your life where you have taken on the self of somebody else or of multiple people and lost your own. So how do you get out of that? Start searching.

I found myself in this position almost a decade ago and I couldn't even tell you the clothes I liked to wear, if I felt pretty in makeup or not, and really what and where a lot of my own beliefs were rooted. This was surprising, because I have always been a strong individual, but at that point I truly did not feel like an individual at all. It took me years to work through, get over and reclaim myself. And even through it, I would always second guess and question if every single decision I made was the right one or if I even liked the decisions I was making. It was such a weird phenomenon and truly is still confusing to me to this day. I remember trying different looks, taking pictures of them and then looking at them to see what I really saw and what I really liked and more importantly where my confidence showed up most.

I remember trying different makeup inspiration with color or neutrals or none, different hair colors or cuts, you name it I tried it. I was constantly waiting for the one moment that something would click, and I would say with complete assurance, this is me. I think I felt so much pressure to hurry and find myself that I just never could. I was stuck in that unhealthy thinking of needing to find myself to prove to somebody else that I did. It goes back to what we previously talked about, that if you are not doing it for yourself and if this is not your journey and your journey alone it will never happen for you and it will never stick. All the while, you are giving that power back to that person or place or thing.

Ironically enough, it actually took me meeting my now husband to ever begin to realize who I was.

Now before you think I found out who I was from him, let me just say it is quite the opposite. Let me also say that you cannot find yourself from anyone else or through anyone else. What happened to me was I found myself in a position that I wasn't pressured to explain myself, justify my likes, or the answer to absolutely every question. I was at a place where I was simply accepted, encouraged, and unconditionally supported and loved.

It was at this time, that I realized there is no pressure to figure it all out and that many times through life, things will come organically in their own way. I finally had the time, freedom and support to take a step back, slow down and be on no one's timeline but my own. I was present with myself every moment of every day and, in a sense, **dated myself. And what a beautiful relationship to invest in and take time for.** I now can tell you the answer to absolutely every question with such strength and confidence and humble contentment because I allowed myself to just be and let myself reveal it on its own time.

During that time, I was lucky enough to be with someone who never questioned that and every time I would find an answer would fuel it with so much love and acceptance for whatever it was. I understand that not everybody may have that, but we do all have time with ourselves and we do need to give ourselves that patience and that support and that love because at the end of the day we're all just trying to figure out who we are. And even when you know who you are, you will and should continue to reemerge and reinvent yourself throughout the years because trust me, you have more to offer and more power to uncover than you would ever believe in your wildest dreams.

We live in a world that so forcibly believes you have to know everything and be everything and check every box and have every plan and be perfect all while doing it. I'll go ahead and ask it; but why? What do we gain by constantly living in this stance of having to explain to ourselves and everyone around us who we are and what we will be and why? Wouldn't it be more prudent to stand in the moment and make the best decisions we can with what we have and where we are in our own growth and allow ourselves to be enough in each and every moment. All the while, still striving for the very best but allowing the answers to come when they are meant to come. Many times, I feel like when we force plans or answers or reasoning it's simply not the right one or just not the best. Everything happens for a reason. Do you sometimes need to go out and get that reason? Absolutely, but if it's time to do that you will know because it will align itself and if it's not time to don't force it. What is meant for you is yours already, no one can take that away.

""

Time is so much better utilized with quality versus quantity. Love is so much better utilized with having it be unconditional rather than have it be on terms. Joy is so much better utilized when it comes organically versus a need to feel happiness at the moment. Your relationship with yourself is the only one that will truly be from the day you start your life to the day it ends. Think about that. Don't take your own relationship for granted assuming you don't have to nourish it and feed it and love it and grow it and even check in with it. Don't lose yourself in this race to find everything else you think you need, and you think comes first. You come first. And there will forever and always only ever be one of you.

I have a love hate relationship with social media. I do not have a Facebook, but I have kept Messenger so I can talk to my family around the country. I have an Instagram, but it is purely for my work and random stories about my kids. Even with that limited portal to the social media world, I can easily find myself getting wrapped up in everything else that is out there. All of the half-truths, filtered reality's, and following influencers in any realm for what is deemed the latest and greatest.

We all do to some degree experience that because we are all human. Sometimes I try to imagine a world without it. When I think about that, I think the first thing that would change is an increase in self-love. It is hard separating reality verse a filtered view. It is hard dealing with the judgments of others who can freely give their opinion to absolutely anybody with no basis, no repercussions for their words, and never having to know or care about that person or situation ever again. It is easy for the cowards of this world to be the strongest people on there.

It is disheartening to see social media utilized for one sided rants and high-horse moments, to play victim to the ways of the world in their own opinions, and just rewarding the mentality of keyboard warriors. The same can be said with the sadness it brings seeing the filtered views of people who know that they look nothing like the pictures they post but still feel this need to have others believe it (and themselves). Dealing with the constant pressure of who is following who and who liked what is a spiral staircase I chose not to climb. What I would encourage you to remind yourself is this, nothing in life is 100% what is seems except yourself, and let's be honest, even that may be not 100% some days. And at the end of the day not one part of any of that matters. Not to your worth, not to your soul, not to your truth, and not to your journey. And if you have been hurt by something on social media, you are stronger than that comment or post.

A saying I often bring up and remind myself of is this, there are two sides to every single story. Life is no different than that. The only time you know 100% of anything is when it pertains to yourself and the crazy thing is what your 100% truth is, may be perceived differently from anybody else's over the exact same situation. That is why being wholly authentic and content with that authenticity is crucial. I can look at Instagram for an hour and get ideas of maybe a different hairstyle or color or outfit or date night idea or even a fun activity to do with my kids. But at the very end of the day, I know beyond that post they are all just trying to figure it out as I am. Every single person struggles with authenticity. Even the strongest most "I am woman hear me roar" people will at points in their life struggle with who they are. With loving themselves. And with feeling completely whole all by themselves and where they are at, at that time. That is why delegating your time, your attention, and your growth to the right things can make the world of difference.

❝

Instead of comparing yourself to others, compare yourself to who you were a year ago or two years ago or even ten years ago (or ten minutes ago).

Look at the growth both internally and externally, or look at the decline, and figure out what caused either one. What made you feel the best out of that time period, what made you feel the worst, why did you make the decisions you made, ask yourself every possible question. Because it's those questions that you see the answers to when you're looking and lusting over other people or other people's lives or other people's situations. Once you have your answers, appreciate where you are at in the moment, but start manifesting the things that are to come. Embrace yourself but continue to grow and enhance it for the purpose of none other than having more passion within that embrace.

Positive Affirmations for both Internal and External Self

- I love being me
- I become a better version of myself every day
- I am unique
- I am whole
- I make a positive difference with the world around me
- I do my very best every day
- I trust myself
- I can do anything I put my mind to. Even the hard stuff
- I am so worthy of love
- I am forgiving
- I get stronger inside and outside every single day
- I am a beautiful work of art
- I am so so brave
- I face my fears with intrigue and grit
- I am talented

CHAPTER SIX

Who is your Jury? What is your Worth?

The fear of judgement in the world of aesthetics and mental health while balancing the cost and whether you're putting it into the right areas

One of my favorite things to discuss is owning mental real estate. What does that mean? If you find yourself doing things because of what other people said to you, acting a certain way because of how you feel based on situations in your life, or finding yourself at every milestone instead of giving yourself the credit for it you see and compare it to the negativity that maybe sparked you to do something.

As an example, say you share a social media post about how wonderful your relationship is but then right after you say all of the negatives. Majority of your words spewing how no one wanted you together, how you were told this or that, and all the other negatives things that over shadow everything positive you said, but hey, look at you now. You are taking away from your joy and milestone. You are giving away your positivity and giving that moment to whoever or whatever made you feel oppressed in that situation. To accomplish something and then immediately pay more attention to any hurt, negativity, or trauma lingering from the very situation, takes away from you owning your own victory and takes away from the joy of it. It also shows that whatever situation or whatever person caused that, owns mental real estate in your brain. They have power over you, they own your victories because you always willingly given it to them, and they own your future because you are making decisions based off of your hurt.

Someone or something "owning mental real estate", is one of the unhealthiest traps that people fall into. Even if absolutely nothing happened but you are just jealous or insecure and feel that you have to do or say certain things to prove some fabricated level of success or happiness that nobody really asked you to prove, you still have given away that mental real estate. Your only jury in life is yourself and your higher power, so please, stop letting other people be that for you!

Your spouse and your family are supporters of you, they are partners with you, they are shoulders and sound boards for you, and though you are walking the same path you all are going to take different turns. The great news? They are not there to judge you or be your jury. Of course, you're going to get advice from them, and guidance and you should trust that they have your best interest at heart but that does not mean that it is where your decisions come from. With that being said you are nobody's jury and you also don't have the power to know what's best truly for someone else and to know what's not a good decision because your view on that decision may be completely different. Of course, there is always a fundamental right and wrong and we should hold one another accountable to that but outside of that it truly all is our own judgment and moral foundation.

I have watched mothers, partners, and friends bring their loved ones in for aesthetic treatments and listen to them go back and forth with what should be done what shouldn't be done. What they should feel bad about what they shouldn't feel bad about and it's truly so damaging especially to women where we are held to an undeniably unrealistic expectation in life, and it does nothing but hold us back. Nobody is helping you by telling you need to change yourself especially aesthetically. Nobody is helping you by telling you something about you is not good enough. Nobody holds the answers or the final decision of truly what is right or what is wrong for you. Only you have that power for yourself.

""

Sometimes your biggest dreams and goals are best kept to yourself and only shared with the right people when they come to life.

I hear so many times the wonderful ideas people have and how they ended up not acting on them because of what their families or loved ones said. We allow people to talk us out of our own purpose when they have their own purpose to worry about. Even with writing this book it took me 3 years of wanting to write it for me to actually write it because I shared a dream with people who shared a different one for me and their words somehow became my reasoning.

Typically this is not malicious. It is not to keep you from anything. A lot of time, it is other people's fear of failure and their want for their idea of what is best for you. The problem with that, is their version of what would be best for you is coming from their perspective and not from your own journey. Even in that best intentions people can talk you out of your purpose. If you feel you have a new path you need to take, a milestone you need to achieve, a dream you just can't let go of, keep that to yourself in hopes of celebrating its reality with the right people when you make it happen.

Sometimes guarding yourself is the best mental health protection you have. Whether someone has good or bad intentions, it is their own intentions and not yours. Only you know the answers to many questions that you are seeking answers for. It is difficult enough to separate sticking to your truth and your journey and your dreams when you are hearing feedback from people with the best intentions but imagine how much harder it would be if you were hearing it from a place of manipulations or ill intention. That could be crippling and potentially stop the path that you were currently on and though you can always get back to it, it may not be the exact same ending that it would have been. Putting your goals and dreams and intentions in the hands of others can come at many costs and typically none of them are as valuable or rewarding as your own.

What is the Cost?

The cost of anything comes into play and can be used for manipulation, as a guilt trip, or as an enticing offer to make the plunge to do something, especially in aesthetics. Money does odd things to people. It can be a means of a way on your aesthetic journey, it can be a derailment to it, but it can also be a cause to more doubt and questions. I have seen husbands guilt trip their wives into feeling bad about spending that money, so they in turn stop taking care of themselves the way that they want to. I have also seen husbands manipulate the situation and push these procedures on their wives simply because they have the money to do so whether the wife truly wants to or just simply wants to appease her husband. I have seen the same thing amongst friends and amongst family. And almost worse than that, we use those very techniques on OURSELVES. Talking ourselves out of things we truly want, discounting our own worth for the sake of some reasoning we have convinced ourselves of, I've seen it all.

I've also seen just as debilitating of a cost coming from very good intentions. I've seen parents want to protect their children from failure so much that they don't see the worth in supporting and encouraging their dreams because they do not have the same confidence in it working out and think they are protecting them from an inevitable failure. I have seen friends stop potentially great relationships out of wanting the best for their friend even though their best doesn't match up with their friends' true best. I have seen coworkers or even acquaintances use their own shortcomings, embarrassments, failures, or doubts with situations that happened to them and project it in a matter of making you feel like it will happen to you. Though those intentions come from a place of love and concern they're just as toxic to your dream, goal, self-care, purpose, and everything in between.

All I can say is know your worth. In regard to aesthetics, if you are looking to get anything done to enhance your already complete self, a price tag should not be your deciding factor. You are worth more than a Groupon code, you are worth more than a bargain, and you are also worth more than doing something you're not sure about.

Take time to meet different providers, see who connects with you on a level that surpasses their before and after pictures, and when it comes to price, budget accordingly. You do not have to do something in the same second you decide you want it. Make your desires happen but make them happen in a way that doesn't then bring stress or regret on your own self judgement and pocketbook. Be very honest with your injector about your wishes, your why's, your expectations, and yes, your budget. A good provider will map out a plan around your budget and goals with a realistic timeline to get you those things even if it means that it is small and slow increments of work overtime. If somebody is pushing you to do everything at once or trying to convince you to maybe take out a line of credit to do so that may not be the best option for you. And who knows, you may not end up wanting everything you thought you would on this slow and steady road. We often think we need more than we do, we often think we want more than we do. And along the way we often realize that the sources of those thoughts of needing and wanting typically are influenced by forces other than ourselves and/or our true desires.

Along the same line of making moves to make what you want in life happen, if you are looking to move forward on a new career path, soul search, or simply want to set boundaries and create a different environment around you, know that you have the complete power to make those choices as well.

This mindset is not just founded in aesthetics. If you feel that something is deep rooted in you and you have that on your heart and you have that in your mind and you're willing to do the work and move forward with it and you believe in it with every inch of your body, there is not one person who can stand in your way if you don't allow them to. People would be in such a higher level of accomplishment whether in a tangible way or intangible if there was even an equal amount of encouragement, support and love as there is doubt and fear and let's be honest, pure haters. Keep going. You are where you are for a reason and you will get to be where you need to be for the reasons you have within yourself that maybe you just haven't uncovered yet, but you will.

"

You have to find the courage to let go when you are no longer being pulled to the energy you want. You have to find the strength to leave when what you want is no longer there. You cannot find your worth in someone else or by proving it. You value is found when you become aware of how worthy you are and what is truly worth your energy.

-Tiffany Moule

CHAPTER SEVEN

Be Deliberate

With every choice, every decision and move you make, make it WITH purpose, ON purpose, and 100% intentional (YOUR intention)

A phrase I say at least once a day in my house is be deliberate and be intentional.

Sometimes I say it so much my kids and my husband get annoyed. But let me tell you, it is the best way to describe being good to yourself. In everything we do, being intentional is a reflection of how we feel about ourselves. If you start tasks that you don't finish, if you rush through tasks without fine tuning them, if you want to be efficient but not effective, or procrastinate, that is a reflection of your own view of self-worth.

Every choice or decision you make is a steppingstone either up or down to your next chapter in life. You must be thorough, efficient, deliberate, and intentional in all things especially the ones that can have an effect on your soul, your well-being, your success, and your relationships. When writing this book, I even thought out how many chapters and how many pages and was very deliberate with the number of each because I wanted to somehow incorporate meaning behind it. I looked up biblical meanings behind numbers, I put together all of our birthdays, I went through every area I could find that would make the number of chapters and each part of this book be deliberate and have a meaning that was powerful to me. It was deliberate and intentional. It may seem silly to some, or even nonsensical but with this book, I wanted every single part of it to mean something. To have purpose. I think I got that from my mother, who anytime any date or event or something as simple as a good report card came around, she was so deliberate and intentional in making sure you felt pride, support, and love in every sense of each of those words. No victory small or large and no milestone for that matter was ever done without extraordinary thought, intent and loving execution which truly drove us to be better, achieve more, and turn around and give that same intensity to the world.

Wouldn't it be something, if we could all view our decisions each and every day like this, simply because we are worth it, and are worth the very best outcome possible? When people come in and they do not know where to start with their journey in aesthetics, that's understandable. But if you come in with no real direction and a mindset of "well just fix me", the result is not going to truly match the expectation because it is unknown. It's almost like when someone asks you what you want to eat, and you say you will eat anything, but then after eating you feel disappointed with what you got. That disappointment is 100% on you for not being intentional and truly checking in with yourself with what would have given you satisfaction. In a very rushed world, with a million things on your plate, you still need to check in with yourself and make sure you are complete and so are your decisions.

When you start holding yourself to such a high standard and demanding your best for yourself each and every day you will be surprised at how quickly you do not tolerate or even entertain less than, from others. You will also be surprised at how accountable you will become if you personally are giving less than, to others or yourself. And that is not to make you feel bad! You should start viewing present weaknesses as future strengths. I get excited when my husband brings something to my attention that maybe I could work on because I know a breakthrough is going to happen, and I know I will conquer it. I know I will be even better and grow even more into somebody I can love at a new level. Finding flaws in yourself is not a negative thing unless you make it. None of us are perfect. Embracing those flaws and enhancing them into a strength whether it be internally or externally can be an exciting adventure and one you should tackle head on.

Speaking of flaws being pointed out, let's quickly touch on the intention behind judgment and learning to read the room or at least the person. Before you take in anything somebody else has to say, before you feel the need to change, grow, take a look at something, please make sure the intention is truly for the better of you and your soul and your journey and you as a person. Because an intention of somebody else's and their view will never reward you with the growth, it will reward them. I know beyond a doubt in my mind, my husband's intentions for me are 100% pure and always with him knowing my goals and my path and wanting to support that. However, I've been in situations where I truly take in suggestions or intentions that others have or think I should have and I've learned to really gut check them and put them against my dreams, my goals, who I am ,what I resonate with and decide if that's a deliberate move in the right direction and on the path that I'm going. I look at if it's a deliberate move on where I should be going and valid feedback, or if it's an intention from their point of view and it doesn't match up with mine. Whether it comes from ill intent or a harmless intent, treat both with respect but let it go as quickly as it came. Of course, anybody is free to give you any advice they want but part of self-growth is learning what to apply and what to let fly and at the end of the day, good bad or indifferent, nobody knows you the way you do.

There is truly nothing in life that happens by mistake. Of course, we make mistakes, but I always view those as the worlds way of working it out the way it should have been all along. At the end of the day what's meant to be, will be. What we can do however is by being deliberate and being intentional in our self-thoughts, in our external actions and everything in between, we can maybe get to that place quicker and without the trauma along the way. Not that it's a race, but wouldn't you want to save yourself the stumbles, the twists and turns, and everything else that may come by just giving yourself 100% from the start. And aren't we also deserving of that? In case you need to hear it, yes you are 100% deserving of giving yourself 100% every day. That includes living by your intention first, and gut checking everything along the way. It is by ultimately going with where that leads you and driving headfirst into your journey unapologetically and with a confident grace daily despite the discomfort it may bring to others who are not ready for that change or not ready for boundaries to be set.

I wanted to do this chapter a little bit differently and instead of just drilling in these words, I wanted to put them into play and show you some ways that you might be doing something on a daily basis that could possibly be done with a little bit more intention for a greater result. We are going to look at ways we start our day, look at ideas to end your night with intention, and checking in with yourself weekly to make sure you are on the right path to be achieving wellness, balance, and on the path of self-love and growth. That is what is going to get you to the place we all deserve and want to be as a whole. You may do every single one of these things already, and if you do that is absolutely amazing. In that case, maybe take a look at what areas you may be lacking that intention or deliberate drive in. It can be easy to fixate on the check lists of what we think we should be doing, but if there are personal things going on with you or individual struggles that maybe you want to deal with, I am going to also try to dive into a few areas that I think may help at the end. Wherever you are at in your journey, know that you are right where you are meant to be right now, and your next steps will dictate the breakthrough and the next stone to stand on. So be deliberate and be intentional and the reward will be your best version of you.

Ideas to start your day in a more deliberate way

- Wake up and take a moment to give gratitude
- Manifest your intentions for the day before you get out of bed, think through your plan of action, your schedule, and how you will execute each thing
- Fuel your body! Your brain needs food (and let's be honest, coffee or tea doesn't hurt)
- Take a moment to yourself whether it be to stretch, to work out, to pray, to read, or even to look in the mirror and recite positive affirmations or where you see yourself in 1 year, 2 year, or 3 years from now.
- Shower, or at least wash your face and PLEASE follow with skin care and sunscreen. During this time, NO negative talk. Focus on only the affirmations and self-love towards your body and reflection.
- Set yourself up to not be rushed in the morning. I know we all love our sleep, but study after study shows starting your day without being rushed and being fully ready and whole before you walk out of the door will lead to better decision making and a better day
- Before you leave, check in with yourself: Do you have everything you need, do you know what you need to accomplish and how to do so, do you feel ready for the day, and of course…are you forgetting anything?
- We all need our phones but let's not check social media if at all possible until after all these steps! Emails and social media are last, not first.

End your night with Intention

- Turn off screens and social 1 hour before bedtime
- Journal or reflect on your highlights of the day, how much you accomplished, your favorite parts, and when you felt best
- Give gratitude for all the moments, all the feelings, and all the opportunities weather positive or not
- What wasn't the best? What could you have done different?
- Did you notice a change in energy or self-reflection around certain individuals, certain situations, or influenced by anything else? If no, was is a positive or a negative. If it was negative, explore that and revisit if you have healthy boundaries in place and ways to avoid taking those negative feelings on
- Set your intent for the next day
- Wind down in whatever way suites you, and pay yourself credit along the way: read, journal, pray, stretch, meditate, take a bubble bath
- Of course, I have to say this, please wash your face!

**Tip: Set your sleep up for success. If there are scents, textures (silk pillow case or thick weighted blanket), or any other factors that would add to your rest and relaxation at night, add it in and enjoy!

Weekly check-in with yourself to
make sure you're on the right path

- Write out your accomplishments, no matter how small
- Write out areas you could have done better, or you'd like to work on
- Did you complete all your intentions this week? Why or Why not?
- How can you better complete them next week?
- How are you feeling about yourself? Have you noticed anyone or thing affecting that in a positive or negative way?
- Did you feel you stayed true to yourself and to your boundaries during the week? If not, why, when, and how do you feel about that now?
- Do you feel you grew or stayed the same?
- Did you treat your external well? i.e., nutrition, physical activity, getting rid of negative self-talk, and keeping up with your aesthetic goals. If not, why, and where did that come from?
- What goals, tweaks, or adjustments do you want to make for next week to further moving forward in your journey?

**Tip: Keep these through the weeks to look back on monthly, or even as the months pass. You may be surprised at how uplifting it can be to see your journey through them. There is something special about being able to look at a tangible record of how far you have come, the struggles along the way, and have an idea on where you are heading.

Ways to Be Deliberate through Healing

- Write out your trauma or areas you need healing from
- Under each event or area, write out these sub areas:
- How do you need to be healed from that? Therapy? Journaling?
- Can you get closure from the event? And If you cannot receive it the way you believe you need it, what are other ways of breakthrough and learning to cope with it and gain self-closer?

Next, what are you triggers?

- How can you avoid them, and if unavoidable, how can you work through them?
- Do you personally possess things, dwell on things, or do things that may be adding to being triggered? i.e. watching a movie with trauma or situations alike then going to bed and having a triggered nightmare

After that, who are your people?

- Where is your support coming from, and have you shared your needs of healing with them so they can help?
- Most Importantly, what can you do through this process to love on yourself, pay yourself respect, and get to know you better?

Last but not least, what does "healing" mean to you?

- What goals do you envision through this?

Ways to be Deliberate through Boundaries

- Stop worrying about how people will feel when you set them!
- Make a list of individuals and situations that you need to make better boundaries with.
- In respect to each of the things previously listed, right out what boundaries you think you need why you need them and how that would improve your space and well-being.
- Role play! If you are concerned that this might cause rift or even arguments, talk yourself through your delivery and put yourself in different situations of how you would handle responses so that you are better prepared to come in with confidence to set your boundaries.
- Stick to them! Doing all of this work is all for nothing if it is not done consistently. This is the new you, this is you valuing yourself and your journey and your Wellness above all, and this is you proving to yourself that all the discomfort was worth it. Stick to your boundaries and do not reevaluate anything for six months or until those individuals develop a respect and understanding for them and come to you to work through whatever issues you had to need to set them in the first place.
- Check in with your own personal boundaries and how you're respecting yourself in ways like being kind to yourself, holding yourself accountable, and sticking to your goals.
- Set up reminders whether it be a note, something on your phone, or some type of picture or item that you can play strategically around your daily schedule to remind you of this path that you were on and of your "whys"

"

You are allowed to hope for what is to come,
while making the most of where you already are
-Morgan Harper Nichols

CHAPTER EIGHT

Where to start? And What Happens After?

What steps do you need to take? And now that you took the leap, how to set yourself up to keep growing, keep thriving, and keep beautifying both on the inside and outside

How do you start this journey? First decide where it needs to begin. Does it need to begin with your own internal healing? Then I would seek out a therapist, a life coach, a group, or even start adding healthy strides to your daily activity such as journaling, meditation, diving into a Bible or higher power of your choice, or something else that is going to heal and bring together balance.

Next, set your intentions. Whether it be intentions internally or intentions externally. Matters of the soul or matters of the eye. Set those and be deliberate and specific with exactly what your goals are. Now manifest them. Speak them out, tell people about it not for opinion or direction, rather, as if it's already happening and be so sure and so confident in your success already that the universe can do nothing but support it. Truly believe that it is already done and meant for you. Now, just do it. Make the needed appointments, meet the needed people, confront the needed trauma, work through and not around everything you need to. Act on it. And act on it with such a purpose and with 100% of yourself and nothing else and nobody else pushing you along the way. You are enough, you can do this, you will succeed.

In regard to injectables and the external aesthetics let's say that is the path you have gone down. Let's say in a perfect world you follow these suggestions, and you make the plunge, and you start your aesthetic journey and now you're at the end of the results and happy, whole, and ready to move forward in life. How do you move forward? What happens after?

One interesting aspect I find is when people get what they want in life they talk themselves into thinking it wasn't enough, there's now not the same level of joy going forward, or more times than not they think that the bar that was set or the expectation that was set wasn't high enough, so they set an even higher one. Let me tell you how none of that benefits yourself or the situation. Though you should always be reaching higher and higher in a sense of bettering yourself and growing and educating yourself more on any area of life, you still need to take a moment to stand in the presence of where you are at. If your goal was to get in shape and enhance some features through aesthetic procedures, and you did that, take a moment and give yourself that glory. Celebrate yourself! Allow yourself to feel good about what you've accomplished and the gift you have given yourself without immediately thinking of what's next. You will never find true peace if you don't allow it to be enough at the moment. Sit in your own beauty, sit in your own accomplishments, sit in your own milestones and give yourself the credit, the time, and the ability to truly soak it in before immediately jumping to the next race.

I have also seen a sort of buyer's remorse after aesthetic procedures whether that be self-doubt, feeling bad for spending money on yourself, thinking that your decision wasn't the right one, a list of things. Most often it comes from the reaction of others when you first do something for yourself and that goes back to owning your own journey. I have been married seven years and to this day I find myself asking my husband if I could buy a new pair of workouts pants or justifying why I have to get my nails done every six weeks or justifying why I'm going to buy a certain skin care line and shopping around until I can find a discount to make it "worth it".

My husband has never once in his life told me not to buy something, told me what to do with money, or ever questioned anything I did for myself. The very opposite he encourages me to do more and to feed my soul in any way I need to. He is truly my biggest supporter and has never once doubted any dream or direction I want to go. But I stand in my own way at times, and I block view of my own worth. I'm human! I don't know why we do that to ourselves, but it needs to stop. If you are intentional and deliberate with your decisions, then they were the right ones. Stand on it and move forward. Also understand that once you reach that goal or once you get that procedure or once you heal that wound, growth never stops.

My dad always told me growing up that education of any kind is the one thing no one can take away from you. This is most likely why I have never stopped in any facet of my life. With every degree, with every milestone, with every feat, he was there to stand with me as I accomplished it and rejoice. To then be there and encourage the possibilities of what could be next. Education of self and our own journey is no different than that of academia. I believe educating yourself should never stop whether it be in the growth of your own self, in your own healing, in learning new things about yourself or learning new ways to find contentment or passion or even new likes or dislikes.

Education doesn't just have to be a vessel to advance you in society or success of a career. We should always be reinventing ourselves without thinking that means that our present self is not already completely and eternally good enough. I would encourage each one of you to never stop learning of new ways to love yourself and of new ways to grow your spirit. I would encourage you to align yourself with like-minded individuals that pour nothing into you but truth, love, support, encouragement, and acceptance. And if there are individuals in your circle who do none of that, you owe no one any relationship or any explanation. Move on. There is not an individual alive, a successful career, or even a situation for that matter, that is worth the cost of your fulfillment in life, your pride in looking back and knowing you truly lived, your happiness with who you are and where you stand, your truth in the same, and above all your love in all astounding areas of it. The more you pour into yourself internally the more of an abundance will be poured onto you externally. The more you will see life is so short but can be a lot more beautiful and fuller than we think, and so can we.

Step by Step Guide:

Grab a piece of paper and Let's Begin!

What are your top 3 Internal Concerns?

What are your top 3 External Concerns?

For Internal:

1. What tools do you need to conquer these?

- Therapist
- Meditation/Journaling/Personal check ins
- Do you need to change, remove, or add something to your personal life by ways of cutting ties with something or someone or removing negative energy or presence in some way? If so, how can you effectively do that without disrupting your personal peace long term?

2. What steps do you need to take to insure this is a character change and not a momentary change?

- How are you going to hold yourself accountable?
- How will you intergrade this into your daily life?
- What do you need to set yourself up for success?

3. Budget and be deliberate with your Time and Cost

- Are there expenses involved in your needs/tool?
- How can you make this work with your budget?

- How can you make this work with your timeline and personal schedule?
- Does insurance cover anything?

4. DO IT!

- Make that first appointment or gather the tools your need to begin
- Mark everything on your calendar, even set reminders on your phone or personal affirmation messages to keep you moving forward
- STAY CONSISTENT. YOU ARE WORTH IT!

For External

1. What tools do you need to conquer these?

- Consultation with provider or professional in that field
- Stylist
- Nutrition/Personal Trainer/Meal Prep Service
- New Skin/body care regimen
- Is something or someone holding you back from these? Do you need to change, remove, or add something to your personal life by ways of cutting ties with something or someone or removing negative energy or presence in some way? If so, how can you effectively do that without disrupting your personal peace long term or hindering you achieving your external goals?

2. What steps do you need to take to ensure this journey is a consistent and successful one?

- How are you going to hold yourself accountable?
- How will you intergrade this into your life and schedule?
- What do you need to set yourself up for success?

3. Do You know Who you need to talk to?

- Do you have reputable sources for your external needs
- Are you budget shopping or quality shopping?
- Look into resumes, before and after's, and do not stop at just one consultation if you have absolutely any doubts or reservations

4. After the consultations, do you feel comfortable and understand everything?

- Take a list of questions and pictures
- Ask them to write down a tangible game plan for you to have to take home
- If you are getting products, ask them to write down the why, how, and when for them

5. Budget and be deliberate with your Time and Cost

- Are there expenses involved in your needs/tool?
- How can you make this work with your budget?
- How can you make this work with your timeline and personal schedule?
- Are there reward programs that can assist in making this more attainable?
- Does insurance cover anything?

6. DO IT!

- Make that first appointment or gather the tools your need to begin
- Mark everything on your calendar, even set reminders on your phone or personal affirmation messages to keep you moving forward
- YOU ARE WORTHY OF TREATING YOU! YOU ARE DESERVING!

List of Yearly check in to plan accordingly

SUGGESTIONS FOR SOUL MAINTENANCE

- Journaling
- Meditation
- Reading
- Connect deeper with your higher power
- Group or individual Therapy

SUGGESTIONS FOR AESTHETIC MAINTENANCE

(General rule of thumb and goals in the medical aesthetics world)

- Quarterly Micro needling with PRP
- Quarterly neuromodulator's
- Yearly filler
- Monthly-bimonthly Facials
- Quality skin care regimen
- Support groups
- Join something that bring you joy and physical/emotional connection with other like-minded individuals
- Budget! Sit down and write out your yearly income, bills, responsibilities, then devote some to growing your passions, your dreams, yourself and fit your wants and mental health/personal needs in there too. There is always room to work in the least of things to validate your worthiness or TLC and self-love. Even if it's just devoting an hour or two a week to taking yourself to coffee or lunch, or on a hike. Make a plan and find a way

"

You might be surprised at who is watching every step of your journey and being inspired by it. Don't give up.
-Unknown

CHAPTER NINE

My personal journey

How Aesthetics healed me

So, what is my story? What does this all mean to me? Aesthetics, for me, has been a very long and exhausting road. With as much pain as it has brought, has come even more joy and beauty. I am truly forever grateful for all the lessons learned along the way. Growing up I was your typical long lean blonde-haired blue/green-eyed little girl. Even as a little girl I remember always being fascinated with ever-changing looks and dressing up. I had big dreams of what I would look like one day, what my kids might look like, and how I would dress as a mom. In my mind, I imagined myself as a famous actress or model. I would never age. Oh, and I would have a million kids, in a complete fairy tale life.

When I was a young girl, I also saw the evil side beauty could bring. I went through certain circumstances that made me hate what others saw as beauty or attractiveness in me. I even thought maybe those circumstances were my fault because of how I looked and resented what I saw in the mirror. When I was a young adult my past trauma and love/hate for what I thought beauty meant lead me to make poor decisions in who I aligned myself with. I attached myself to a partner who I believed was what I deserved, and all I was worth. Though I believe this individual was just as broken as me, there is never an excuse for what went on in that relationship. It truly broke me and took everything I had salvaged of myself with it.

Shortly after, when I was 23, I was assaulted, and it led me to getting reconstructive surgery. I remember afterwards feeling I had lost anything left of who I was even on the outside now. I remember the hardest thing about it was I still had hope one day I would find my happily ever after and one day I would be a mom and my greatest fear was seeing my child with my features and feeling so a part of them but them not seeing their features in me any longer. When I got pregnant with my son, he looked exactly like me from our very first ultrasound and to this very day. I was so embarrassed that if I said that to anyone while I was pregnant, they wouldn't see it since those features had been altered. It wasn't until he was almost 4, one day, he told me that we were Twins. I remember asking him why he thought that and feeling scared of his response and he looked at me and though he did say because we both have straight hair, he looked at me and just said because we are kind, and we are strong, and we are Twins. It was at that time that I realized having the same features as somebody has very little to do with the precise aesthetics of any face or body. He will always be a reflection of me, my twin, and mirror me because of who he is and who I am.

It was at that time I stopped worrying that my kids might ask what a scar was from or why I may respond to things the way I do or all of the little things I thought would be such an issue. Because those who love you will see none of that and the more you love yourself you won't either.

For me, my internal journey through aesthetics was the most challenging period and if we are being honest, is still one I struggle with today. There was a lot of trauma, a lot of hurt, and a lot of self-hate that I had to work through. I still have to be intentional and deliberate every single day. I must choose my happiness, choose this life, and choose the miracle and beautiful masterpiece that it is. But it is a choice I am grateful to be able to make each and every day no matter how hard, no matter the reminders, no matter the moments that stop me in my tracks. I will always choose wellness and hope and grace. I never thought I was deserving of the life or happiness I have now, but I always hoped one day I would see myself as being so, because I knew my strength and I knew if I could see it, it would happen. And happen it did. I have gone from thinking that I was put here to love and just not chosen to be loved, to knowing and waking up to two little perfect faces and one extraordinary man who love me with such force and so unconditionally I have no choice but to be engulfed to it. And every morning when I take a chance to look at myself, I am whole, I am complete, and on my worst day I am beyond enough. We are all deserving of this.

I did not truly appreciate my journey of aesthetics until I was healed from my own trauma and self-hate and only then moved forward to the fine-tuning of the external. I knew I wanted to be able to do things simply to make me feel even better, enhance certain things, and just as maintenance for anti-aging. Many people may say I don't need anything, some people may think I need a lot more than what I get done. But neither positive nor negative feedback will ever hold weight on my personal decisions. I have learned to love the beauty I see in myself without needing to meet a standard of others. I am still learning to appreciate complements without it making me feel like something else is coming and without allowing myself to need them.

Aesthetics can be a beautiful journey. Whether it be soaking in a bathtub, meditating in a beautiful place and feeling one with nature, or enjoying the beauty of our world and just standing in it. It can be treating yourself to a spa day or treating yourself to a procedure that will enhance your own beauty. It can truly be anything internally or externally that amplifies the beauty you already have within you, but when it is looked at as a cure all, it will never be appreciated the same and you will never feel the beauty of true self-care. At the end of the day. We are all in some way broken. Chipped, or with a piece or two missing. Looking for what our glue is to piece us together. Yet know, we are still valuable, still of worth, still fit for use. And some of us, some of us are shattered. Possibly beyond repair or of any use in the eyes of those who had a hand in that breakage or in those who simply can't see the finale and victory past the hill. And yes, the glue may not heal to perfection, and the time and road to get back to a foundation may seem impossible. But let us not forget, the shattered ones, those are the only ones when held up, that the brightest light shines through.

The Velveteen Rabbit

"Real isn't how you are made," said the Skin Horse. "It's a thing that happens to you."

"Does it hurt?" asked the Rabbit.

"Sometimes," said the Skin Horse, for he was always truthful. "When you are Real you don't mind being hurt sometimes."

"Does it happen all at once, like being wound up," he asked, "or bit by bit?"

"It doesn't happen all at once," said the Skin Horse. "You become. It takes a long time. That's why it doesn't happen often to people who break easily, or have sharp edges, or who have to be carefully kept. Generally, by the time you are Real, most of your hair has been loved off, and your eyes drop out and you get loose in the joints and very shabby. But these things don't matter at all, because once you are Real you can't be ugly, except to people who don't understand."

"Once you are real you can't become unreal again. It lasts for always."

"Once we come into our self, our real selves, we're able to hold onto ourselves, and you cannot go back,"

"When you know what it feels like to be unconditionally loved, you can't undo it or un-experience it."

WORDS TO LIVE BY

Here are some truths to read, stand on, and live by. Write them on your mirror, add them to your screen saver, engrave them in your heart.

"

You are enough

"

Your power comes from your reflection, not your reaction

"

Never dim your own light in hopes of making someone else's shine brighter. And be mindful of the same happening to you

"

You are wholly capable and fully in charge of who you are and where your path may lead you

"

Though you are a complete, unique, masterpiece, you have all the power to enhance your inner and outer being in any way you may chose

CPSIA information can be obtained
at www.ICGtesting.com
Printed in the USA
LVHW020227130421
684331LV00006B/273